Moment for Morricone

for Clarinet Quartet

Music from "The Good, the Bad and the Ugly"
and "Once upon a time in the West"

E. Morricone

28
p
p
mf
32
Più mosso
f
f
f
f
3
3
3
3
37

58
sfz
sfz
p
p
63
Empty
68
pp
pp
pp
fp

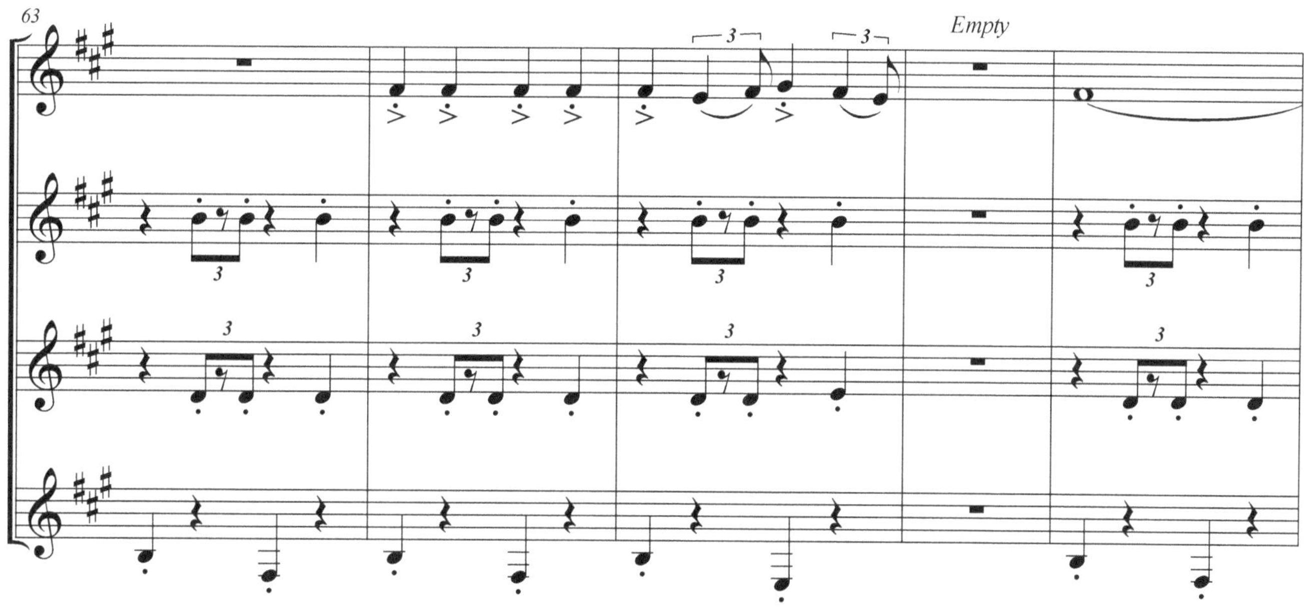

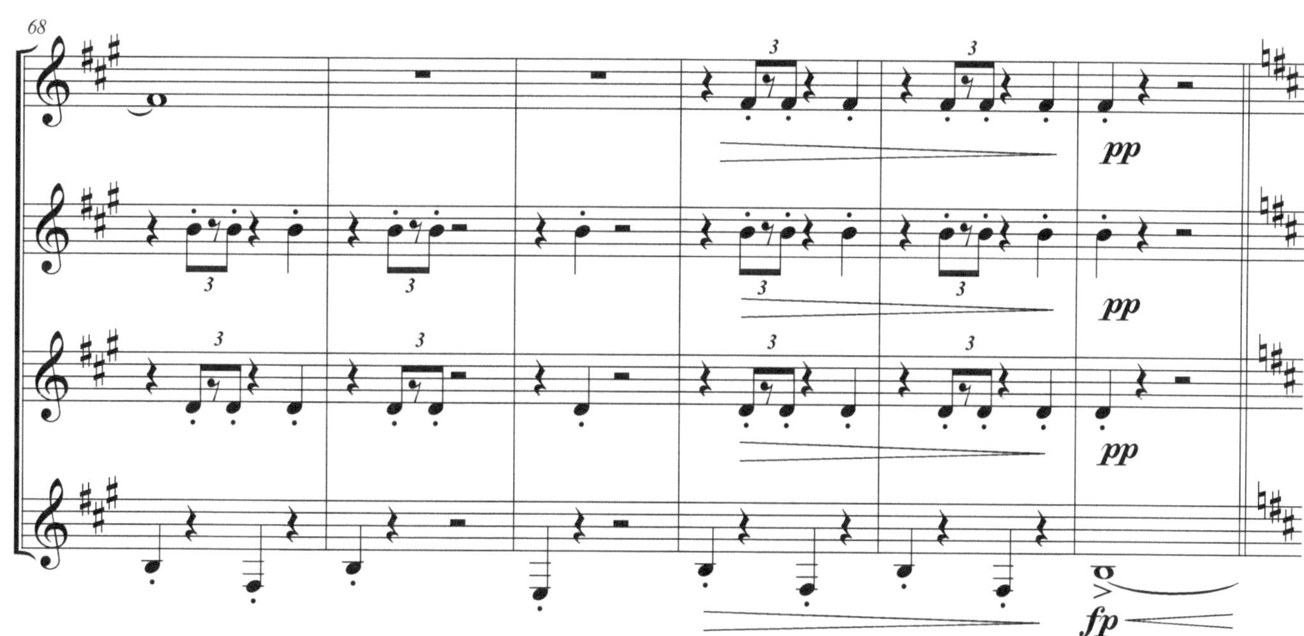

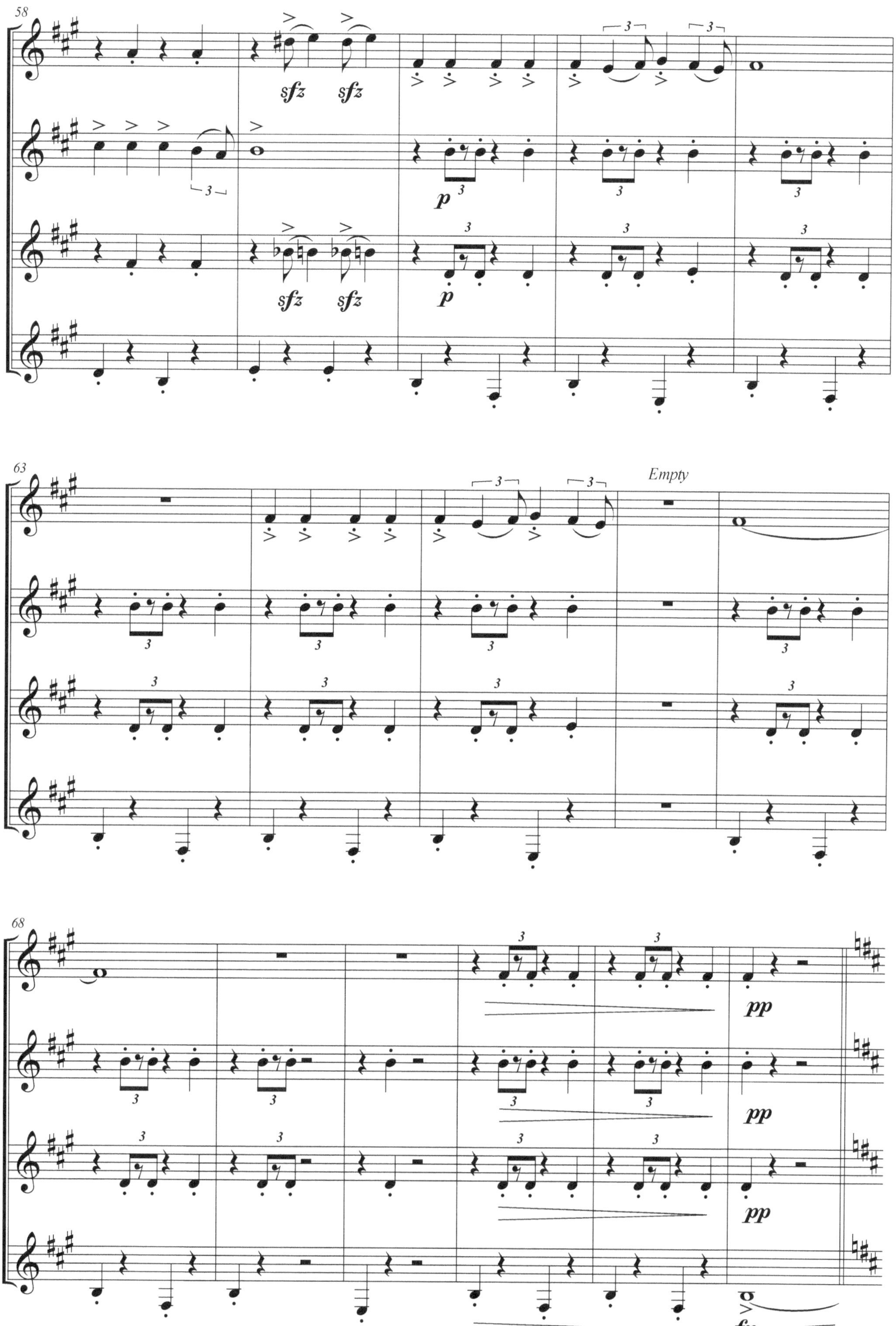

131
rit.
Grandioso
135
f
f
ff
f
3
3
139

142
Vivace
145
148

Moment for Morricone

for Clarinet Quartet
Music from "The Good, the Bad and the Ugly"
and "Once upon a time in the West"

E. Morricone

Moment for Morricone

for Clarinet Quartet

Music from "The Good, the Bad and the Ugly"
and "Once upon a time in the West"

Moment for Morricone
for Clarinet Quartet
Music from "The Good, the Bad and the Ugly"
and "Once upon a time in the West"

Moment for Morricone

for Clarinet Quartet

Music from "The Good, the Bad and the Ugly"
and "Once upon a time in the West"

E. Morricone

114
121
127
132
rit.
Grandioso
f
138
p < f
144
Vivace
p
p
148
ff